The Code of the Warrior

The Code of the Warrior

Daidoji Yuzan

D. E. Tarver
www.detarver.com

Writers Club Press
New York Lincoln Shanghai

The Code of the Warrior
Daidoji Yuzan

Writers Club Press
an imprint of iUniverse, Inc.

For information address:
iUniverse, Inc.
2021 Pine Lake Road, Suite 100
Lincoln, NE 68512
www.iuniverse.com

ISBN: 0-595-26917-6

Printed in the United States of America

Commit to study acts of bravery and valor; emulate them. Do not cast your life away as a coward. One way or another death will come. Determine now how you will face it.

—Daidoji Yuzan

This book is dedicated to all the warriors who have given their lives for the safety and wellbeing of others on battlefields, mean streets, and burning buildings. Whether you have sacrificed life and limb or spent your life in the service of others, may God bless and have favor on you.

Contents

From the Author

Daidoji Yuzan originally wrote the *Budo Sho Shinshu*, literally *Bushido for Beginners*, as a textbook on warrior ethics for young people born into the warrior caste. He wanted to teach them the code of conduct that had long guided the paths of countless warriors. In this translated version, *The Code of the Warrior* maintains the same approach. Some of the beliefs and philosophies of the sixteenth-century Japanese warrior may seem out of step with today's weekend martial artist, but they are completely relevant for today's warriors. Whether you read this book to gain historical perspective or to adopt a code of conduct for your own life, *The Code of the Warrior* will benefit you in many ways. One of those ways is listed in the opening quote: "One way or another death will come. Determine now how you will face it." Although this subject may seem unpleasant, it is a fact that we all must deal with and it is important for you and those you leave behind that you are prepared.

The Code of the Warrior asks us to face the very nature of humanity and to strive to live up to the highest of ideals. Loyalty, Faith, and Bravery make up the foundation for the teaching throughout the book. It is obvious that Yuzan wanted to inspire the younger generation to strive for the things that still elude even the most noble of human beings, especially today in a society that bases much of its education on situational ethics. There is nothing situational about bushido. Right is right and wrong is detestable. Honor is more important than life, and duty more important than comfort. Loyalty and faith are worth sacrificing your life for, and greed is a weakness. We live in a world that teaches one to value personal worth in terms of money, and where heroism is a second-rate substitute. The warrior path is one of self-sacrifice and discipline. Whatever level you aspire to reach, you will find the guidance and instruction here to help you live a life beyond common reproach.

Throughout history, the public has vacillated in its opinion of warriors—they have been seen as a necessary evil and as celebrated saviors. The only constant thing that determined how well they were treated was whether or not the people felt the threat of a dangerous enemy. I believe the American people, especially the grass-roots majority, have always proudly supported the military (not to say that everyone in the military is a warrior). However, for many the military is seen as the last resort of the poor, impoverished, and uneducated. This attitude shows through in people's humor, such as when people call the phrase "military intelligence" an oxymoron. The idea of honor and living by a code is so foreign to most of America that it is relegated to the realm of outdated romance, as in tales like *Don Quixote*. It seems that the same was true in large part during Yuzan's time. Although the people were locked in a caste system, he worried about the lack of understanding and appreciation for the way of the warrior. There are segments of our society today—largely wealthy extremist liberals—who loathe the mere existence of the military.

War comes and goes, but the heart of the warrior beats on. Whether enlisted in the military or not, the burning desire to protect is one of the things that separate us from the sedate, self-infatuated crowd. We are almost a paradox. We strive to improve ourselves so we can insure that others have a peaceful life. We put our lives on the line and feed our children with food stamps. Do not take my references to the military as a suggestion that all warriors should enlist, though many of us find our home there. It's the heart that matters, and it's the spirit that determines who and what we are. Warriors are needed in everyday civilian life as much as anywhere else, but we should recognize our kinship across all career paths.

There is a special place in my heart, and there always has been, for those who choose to fulfill their calling in the service. Having served myself, the brotherhood of Marines has been a real and important influence in my life. Semper Fi!

Enjoy the book. Heed the advice of our ancestors. Seek Truth. To all warriors, in every walk of life, salutations.

D. E. Tarver

About the Writer and the Book

The writer, Daidoji Yuzan, was born a *ronin* (a samurai without a master) in 1635. His family name came from a temple in the family's home town. The time in which he was born seems to be somewhat of a renaissance, especially for the warrior, strategist, and writer. Musashi, Yagyu, and Tsunetomo either wrote or dictated their famous works in or close to this time. We don't know a lot about Yuzan's life other than that the fact he was an avid martial arts student and that he was obviously concerned about the education of the warrior youth. He spent several years traveling the country teaching martial arts and bushido. When he grew too old to travel and lecture, he scribed this work in order to pass his teachings and observations on bushido on to future generations. The work was very popular and was copied many times over. It became the standard text on the subject for youth. At the time of publication, Japan was well into its period of isolation and peace, which left most young warriors longing for a sense of purpose. Some dabbled in commerce and others simply lazed their way through the day doing as little as possible to get by. The *Budo Sho Shinshu* filled a void for many young warriors and set many back on a fevered path of militarism.

Anyone who wants to understand the Japanese mindset today should start with this book. Although the caste system has been long-since abolished, the principles of bushido still influence every facet of Japanese thinking. You will see many similarities between the demanded respect and protocol of bushido and seemingly trivial things, such as accepting a business card with both hands and securing it in a place of honor. If you have ever felt frustrated by the stringent routine of daily life in Japan, this book will help you better understand the long traditions that support many of the seemingly pointless formalities. For instance, it is expected for a person to refuse an offer (of, let's say a meal, for example) three times before accepting. If you offer a Japanese business associate a meal he will probably say "no thank you" whether he wants to go or not. It is your responsibility to talk him into it by urging him several times. This particular situation is not addressed in the book, but the spirit of politeness and the disdain for greed are.

Although Yuzan ends the work abruptly, I believe that the last line really sums up the entire thrust of the rest of the book: "It is the purity of the warrior spirit that is important."

I have divided this text into three sections. The first section deals generally with preparation for active service by addressing such issues as education, equipment, and duty. The second section focuses generally on keeping your home life in order and running smoothly. The last section deals with the concepts and principles of faithful service to one's lord.

Section One:
Preparation for Service

DEATH

One who claims the title of warrior should understand that it is his foremost duty to keep death ever in his mind, from the first moment of New Year's Day to the last moment of the last day of the year.

The warrior who does this will always fulfill all obligations of loyalty and filial piety, avoid a windfall of evils and disasters, and live a long, healthy life. His spirit will grow strong and Heaven and earth will favor him.

A man's life is as fleeting as the evening dew or the morning frost, and a warrior's life is even more uncertain. A warrior who believes that he will live a long life will get caught up in his own desires and may fail to fulfill his duty to his lord or his parents.

Always remember, just because life is here today is no guarantee that it will be here tomorrow. Receive your orders from your lord or parents as though you will never see them again, and you will serve them from a heart of sincerity. This way you will never fall short of total loyalty or filial piety.

Now, the warrior who dismisses death from his thoughts will grow negligent and careless. He will speak without thinking and will say things that offend others and cause arguments. He will contend over issues that should be ignored and cause quarrels and hard feelings. Even in his leisure time, while taking a casual stroll or sightseeing, he is apt to run into some fool and get into a fight. He may even be killed in a brawl and bring shame on his lord and family, all because he did not remember that death is ever-present.

The warrior who keeps death in the forefront of his thoughts will know the power of his words, whether he is speaking or answering others, and will not engage in pointless arguments. He will not allow himself to be lured to undesirable places where confrontation may wait even if he is earnestly beckoned. This is how he will avoid a windfall of evils and disasters.

Regardless of rank, a warrior who lets death slip from his thoughts will eat and drink too much and will become indulgent and lazy. He will become unhealthy and will die before his time, and even as he lives, he is useless.

The warrior who keeps death in his mind even when he is young will live a long, healthy life free of sickness and disease, because he will avoid excesses in food, drink, and sexual addictions.

One who believes he will live a long life and pushes death away from him will be consumed with various lusts and desires. He will covet the property of others and will be consumed with greed. In this he will be no better than a farmer or merchant. Holding death in mind forces one to see the world as fleeting, and this naturally destroys greed and does away with a selfish spirit. This is why I say one's character is improved.

Keeping death in mind does not mean one should sit around all day waiting for it, like Shinkai, the monk that Yoshida Kenko wrote about in *Tsurezuregusa*. This may be fine for a monk, but it will not do for a warrior, who must constantly train in martial disciplines and carry out the various duties of loyalty and filial piety.

A warrior should carry out his daily duties with all diligence and singleness of mind, and meditate on death during moments of rest. It is written that Kusunoki Masashige told his son Masatsuta, "Make death your companion." These words are for the benefit of warriors.

EDUCATION

The warrior reigns over the other classes of society, therefore it is incumbent upon him to educate himself in a wide variety of things in order to better administer his duties.

That said, warriors who were born in times of strife were expected to take sword in hand and engage fully in combat by the age of fifteen or sixteen. Because of this, it was necessary for a young warrior to begin his martial-arts training by the age of twelve or thirteen. They were so busy preparing for combat that few ever had time to properly learn reading or writing, and many went uneducated. This is not to say that they didn't desire to learn these things or that their parents had neglected them, but the martial arts were their only concern because their lives would soon depend on their prowess in this area.

As for warriors born in times of peace, there is no excuse. It goes without saying that warrior children should always train in martial arts, but since there is no immediate threat to their lives, they should start learning classic literature and penmanship by the age of seven or eight. When they reach the age of fifteen or sixteen they should broaden their martial-arts education by practicing archery, horsemanship, and various other arts of war.

In times of peace, there is no excuse for a young warrior to go uneducated. This is not the responsibility of the child; it is incumbent upon the parent to insure that their child learns these things. A parent who truly loves their children will see to their education.

FILIAL PIETY

It is a fundamental duty of the warrior to fulfill his filial duty. Regardless of his looks, intelligence, or abilities, if a warrior is lacking in the care of his parents, he is worthless.

The way of bushido is to know the root from the branch and to act in accordance with propriety. One who cannot tell the root from the branch will not know right from wrong, and one who does not know right from wrong can in no way claim the title of warrior. Understand that your parents are the root of your life just as you are the branches of their flesh, blood, and bone. Those who get carried away trying to make a name for themselves may start to neglect their parents, who gave them life in the first place.

There are two different kinds of parents that must be cared for:

The first are parents who raise their child with kindness and love. They sacrifice for their child and provide them with the best education and the best weapons and training, they find him a good mate, and they leave him a grand inheritance.

There is nothing remarkable about a son remaining loyal to such parents. One would feel the same loyalty for an absolute stranger who had been as kind to him. For such a stranger one may even suffer harm to bring him good, so how much more would he do for a loving parent. Children of such parents can never go too far to the extreme to fulfill their filial duty. This is simply repaying a debt and is only just.

The second type of parent is just the opposite. They are not kind, but cranky, complaining, stingy people who refuse to release any inheritance and constantly press their children to the point of harm while continually criticizing them before others. Such difficult parents as these are still due filial piety from their children, and being able to fulfill such duty to parents like these without showing the slightest annoyance is the true measure of a warrior.

Such a warrior truly understands the spirit of loyalty and when in the service of a master will remain loyal whether the lord is rich or his power has dwindled away. If ninety of a hundred warriors forsake their lord he will remain strong, and of the final ten he will be the last one standing beside his lord, no matter how heavily enemies attack.

A parent and a lord are different, and duty and loyalty are different, but a warrior's responsibility to all of them is the same. There is a saying of the scribes, "Look for loyal warriors among faithful children." It is impossible for a disloyal child to become a loyal servant to his lord. A man who will not show filial piety to the very origin of his life will in no way feel an obligation to his lord, whom he serves only for benefit.

A man who is not faithful to his parents will only serve a lord so long as it benefits him. He will run away in the midst of a battle, and history has proven that such a one will even conspire against his lord for gain.

What a shame.

TWO AREAS OF PREPARATION

For the warrior, there are two levels of readiness and four areas of preparation.

The two levels are normal conditions and combat readiness. The four areas are bushido, martial arts, military law, and military strategy.

Normal bushido requires bathing morning and night, always keeping your hands, feet, and body clean, shaving and dressing your hair every morning and being sure to dress appropriate to the season. Carry your fan and swords in your belt at all times, treat everyone courteously and with the respect due their rank, and avoid pointless chatter. Never take a single bite of rice or a sip of tea without observing proper manners, and always avoid uselessness. Even if you are off duty or resting you should be reading a book or practicing your writing. Never waste your time lounging around lazily. Always recount heroic stories of old, or meditate on the fulfillment of bushido. Above all, it is important to remember that regardless of your activity you should always exemplify the highest standards of conduct expected of a warrior.

Combat readiness for the warrior places first the study of the sword, then the spear, the horse, archery, guns, and other forms of combat. It is the duty of the warrior to master the arts of killing so that he will be ready any time he is called into action.

Discipline yourself to fully understand the areas of ordinary conditions and combat readiness, and you will have the reputation of a reliable warrior worthy of trust and responsibility.

The main purpose for all warriors is to serve in times of strife. During these times, a warrior sets aside his normal activities and changes his normal titles to military titles, such as general and soldier. Regardless of rank, all warriors put their civilian clothing away and don armor, take the sword in hand, and charge the enemy lines. This is the area of military law, and every warrior must be familiar with it.

Lastly, there is the area of military strategy. When you and your allies confront an enemy in battle, you will win if your battle plans and strategy are correct, otherwise you will lose. This area of strategy is very old and is known as the art of war. It is imperative that warriors understand this area of strategy.

A warrior proficient in all four of these areas is the highest level of warrior. A warrior who is proficient in only two of them can still be effective, but he should not hold a post of high leadership.

The path of a warrior requires him to diligently study all the areas of ordinary conditions and combat readiness without ceasing, until he becomes an ideal warrior.

THE IMPORTANCE OF THE SWORD

It is essential for the warrior to remain in the spirit of combat every minute of every day, regardless of his activity.

Our nation is different from others in that everyone, even the lowest farmer or merchant, understands and respects the sword and carries a weapon, even if it's only an old rusty dagger. This is in our nature as a warrior people, even though the other three classes are not warriors by profession.

Now, if even the lowest peasant carries a sword, how much more should a full-fledged warrior determine to never let a second pass without his swords at his side? A true warrior will not so much as take a bath without at least a wooden sword with him. And if one is supposed to be this tenacious about his swords in his own home, how much more so when he is leaving his house? You never know when or where you may run into a fool or drunk who will force you into a fight. As the old saying goes, "When you leave your gate, your enemy is in your face."

As a warrior in a position of responsibility you should never be without your swords—do not let down your guard. If you keep this practice you will fulfill the principle of keeping death foremost in your mind.

A warrior carrying two swords but lacking the spirit of combat readiness is no more than a peasant with swords.

WARRIORS AND PRIESTS

For a long time now, there as been the term "Priest-warrior." It doesn't take much thought to see how alike these two really are.

For example, the followers of Zen use the titles zasu and shuso for low-ranking priests the same way low-ranking warriors are assigned menial tasks. As priests are promoted they are given titles like tanryo and seido just as warriors are promoted to positions such as officer, captain, and commander.

Now when the same priest wears colorful robes and carries symbols of power, he is looked at differently and has power over other priests just as a warrior will have his own banner and uniform and carry the baton of a commander. Such a warrior commands others in battle just as the priest has power over other priests.

Priests and warriors are very similar in their command structure, but when it comes to training, the priests are far superior. As a regular course of training, young priests travel the countryside studying at all the great temples and learning from a great many acclaimed scholars. As they learn and achieve promotions they continue to practice meditation and pursue learning, even after they reach such prestigious positions as the head of a temple. They spend their entire lives studying and pursuing excellence.

I desire the same for warriors, but unfortunately, even beginning warriors earn a comfortable living before ever receiving an assignment. Many have no need of more food, better clothing, or housing, and find themselves married and raising children while still young. They settle into a routine of taking a nap every morning and afternoon and neglect even basic martial-arts training, much less higher levels of strategy and tactics. In this manner they let their lives slip past them as their hair turns gray and they grow bald.

Once one takes on the look of a respectable master he may find himself promoted to a position for which he is not prepared. In such a case, one would have to rely on advisors and councilors just to get through the day. Then, if he is promoted to an even higher post, he must constantly study old books and seek the advice of others to perform the basics of his job. This is unacceptable for the warrior.

The various assignments of a warrior remain unchanged. Rather than spending your time doing nothing while you are young, you should study for the future. Borrow old books and manuals, ask questions of those around you and pay attention to everything that is said, even in passing conversation. Ask questions, take notes, and copy books for future use. Take the time to prepare in advance and you will be ready for whatever may come your way.

Under ordinary circumstances one may well be able to get by with advice from advisors and counselors, but what happens in a time of emergency when one is forced to make decisions on the spot?

A military planner must know the size of armies, the weapons available and the battle array, the strength of forts, the particulars of terrain, and the likelihood of victory. This has been true for many years and it is known as a difficult job. Mistakes by a planner may come from miscalculations or misinformation, and it may cause the commander to risk the lives of his men, which is a great responsibility that he must consider. Both of these posts are vital, and for a warrior to take a job like this that he is unprepared for is a disgrace.

Imagine a priest who has no knowledge of his religion, yet because he is old and wears colorful robes, he is placed in charge of others. If the priest makes a mistake he will be looked at as a fool and dismissed without harm, but a commander who does this will be responsible for many deaths.

Understand this and take the time to prepare while you are young. Discipline yourself and study now so that you are always ready to fulfill any duty assigned to you.

GOOD AND EVIL

The survival of bushido depends on the warrior knowing the difference between good and evil and desperately clinging to all that is good.

Good and evil are essentially the same as right and wrong. Good is right. Evil is wrong. It seems simple enough to understand yet most people do not have the discipline to follow the path of good, because evil is seen as easy, profitable, and more fun. Those who believe this embrace evil and ridicule good as weakness.

It is one matter for a retarded person who cannot tell right from wrong, but it is entirely another for a person of sound judgment to openly turn his back on righteousness. Such a person can never rightly claim the title of warrior because he has no self-discipline, and a lack of self-discipline flows from the heart of a coward.

It is necessary for a warrior to fight against evil and exemplify goodness. There are three levels of goodness.

Let's say a friend comes to you before going on a long trip and has a large sum of money. He says that it would worry him to carry it with him and asks you to keep it safe while he is gone. You agree and your friend sets out. Before he returns you receive word that he has died of food poisoning or a heart attack and no one knows about the money he left with you.

The highest level of warrior would not even give it a second thought, but would immediately contact the man's nearest relative and hand over the money.

The next level of warrior would reason to himself that the man had not really been a very good friend, and since no one knew about the money no one would come looking for it. If such a person were poor he might be tempted to keep the money. But then if the temptation brings intense shame to the man and causes him to change his mind so that he returns the money out of guilt, he is said to have upheld righteousness out of a sense of shame.

The last level warrior is one who returns the money only because someone else knows about it, such as his wife or children. Even though this one has questionable morals, at least he returned the money because he was afraid of what others might think.

A child does what is right out of shame of what his parents or friends will think of him if he does not. Later, as he grows, he does right out of dread of what will become of his reputation if he does not. After a while the habit of following good becomes so ingrained in him that he truly and deeply desires to follow what is right and cannot stand the thought of committing evil.

This lesson also applies to martial valor. One who is born with valor of heart will march unflinching through a hail of arrows and bullets with no sign of fear. Such a warrior is completely devoted to loyalty and duty and will not hesitate to use his own body as a shield. There is no more beautiful sight than to see this type of warrior in action.

But let us consider the man who is not born with a heart of valor and grows faint and weak-kneed in battle. His natural tendency is to hide, but when he sees the brave warrior advancing, his sense of shame compels him to advance also. Even though this type is not naturally brave from the start, over time he can become accustomed to these actions and stand equally with the most valiant warrior.

When you get right down to it, a strong sense of shame can mold a person into an honest and heroic warrior. Those who have no shame do not care that others disdain them and call them cowards. They are beyond hope, and useless.

THE THREE ESSENTIALS

There are three necessary qualities for one who claims the title of warrior. They are loyalty, righteousness, and courage. Now, there are warriors who are loyal, and warriors who are righteous, and warriors who are courageous; but a warrior who embodies all three of these is said to be perfect. Among thousands of warriors it is almost impossible to find even one who fits this description.

Loyal warriors and righteous warriors are easily spotted because their everyday conduct shows their nature; but many doubt that one can spot courage so easily in times of peace. I believe that courage is easily spotted. It does not show up for the first time when the warrior dons his armor and takes a spear in hand to do battle. A courageous warrior will have a courageous heart and it will show through in his everyday conduct and in his loyalty to his lord and parents. He will use his free time to study and will continually practice the martial arts. He will avoid pampering himself and will refuse to waste money. This does not mean that he is stingy, for if he believes in a cause he will give everything he has to support it. He will avoid any place or activity that displeases his lord or parents, even if he is tempted. He will stay fit and healthy in hopes of one day performing some heroic act of self-sacrifice. He will not indulge in food or drink and he will not let the powerful lure of sex control him. Self-control and moderation are the marks of a courageous warrior.

As for the coward, he will show respect to his lord or parent's face, but will disrespect them behind their backs. He cares only for himself. Self-indulgence and extravagance are his gods, and he will follow them regardless of his lord's laws or his parent's wishes because pleasure is first in his life. He is lazy and slothful, sleeping late in the morning and napping in the afternoon. He hates to study, so he is ignorant. He learns the language of the martial arts and boasts of great prowess, although he is weak and has no self-discipline and he cannot perform what he speaks. He wastes all of his money on elegant meals and borrows without concern for the future. With all of his extravagance, he will not so much as repair the armor or saddle passed down to him from his father. He becomes sickly because he overeats and indulges in all sorts of immoral sex. He has no heart or self-control. He is useless to his lord and is the highest form of coward.

This is why I say that courage or cowardice is easily spotted in a warrior.

MORE IS EXPECTED OF THE WARRIOR

The ideas of loyalty and filial piety are not exclusive to the warrior class. Farmers, artisans, and merchants also understand and treasure these values. Manners in the lower classes are not stressed however, and a youth may speak to his mother or father while sitting crossed legged, with his hands in his kimono or flailing about. These things are perfectly acceptable among these classes so long as the youth holds his superior in high regard and does not display an arrogant or disrespectful attitude.

But bushido requires both an internal feeling of respect and the proper manners and courtesies to show it. Either one without the other is insufficient. The slightest neglect in this duty is unacceptable for anyone who claims the title of warrior, even if his parents or lord is away and will never know.

At night, as the warrior sleeps, he must make sure that his feet never point in the direction of his lord, even briefly. With weapons, make sure your sword or spear is never stored so that the point is toward your lord; and when practicing archery, never set up your targets in the same direction as your lord's house.

A warrior engaged in any conversation, whether listening or speaking or overhearing others, should sit straight and tall whenever the lord is mentioned. Never speak of your lord or read a letter from your parents while lounging around lazily, and never disrespect a letter from your parents by casting it about or using strips of it to clean pipes or repair lampshades.

A person who claims the title of warrior and does not follow such principles does not understand the responsibilities of his title. Such a one is likely to gossip about his lord when meeting others out somewhere, and they are quick to spread rumors about their siblings or parents simply to gain the sympathy of some sweet-talker.

A person like this is sure to meet due punishment from their superiors, or karma will return calamity to his door, maybe in the form of a dishonorable death. Even if they live a long life it will be one of turmoil and confusion, certainly not the life befitting a warrior. In the end he will die worthless.

During the Keicho period there lived a brave warrior named Kani Saizo, formally a commander of troops, serving as a keeper of the gate at the Hiroshima Castle. Between shifts he would take naps, because he was very old. One day, a young page of Lord Masanori came to him with a pheasant caught by the lord's bird of prey.

"Lord Masanori sent this as a gift," the young page announced.

Saizo jumped to his feet and quickly dressed without speaking. Then, after he was properly prepared, he received the gift. Afterward he said to the page, "You are a foolish young man. It was your duty to announce beforehand that you'd brought a gift from the lord so that I could properly prepare before hearing it, thus receiving it with due respect. If you were under my charge I would have you punished, but since you are not I will dismiss this error because you are young and ignorant."

The page was shocked, and he hurried away and told his friends about the incident. Before long, Lord Masanori heard of it and called the page before him. After questioning him further the lord said, "Saizo was right to scold you. I wish that all of my warriors were like him, for then we could accomplish anything."

RIDE THE BEST HORSE

In olden days, the ideas of archery and horsemanship were inseparable, but nowadays warriors place their first priority on swordsmanship, then spear, and lastly horsemanship. After these, young warriors commonly practice archery, guns, Iai Jitsu, and hand-to-hand grappling. It is important to study these things while still young, because it is more difficult to learn them when you are old.

In my opinion, it is important for young warriors to learn excellent horsemanship skills, especially those of lower ranks. Gentle, well-trained horses are very expensive and tend to belong to those of high rank. But a lower-ranking warrior can make up what is lacking in his horse with his own riding skills. This way, if you find a horse that is perfect but for one flaw, such as if it is high-spirited or has bad habits, you can purchase it very cheap and can ride a horse that is of a caliber above your rank.

For the most part, only those of high rank or means can reject a horse simply because of its color or coat. A warrior of more meager means would be foolish to refuse an otherwise fine horse based solely on its color or coat.

There was once a commander named Kakuganji in charge of about three hundred horsemen in the service of the Murakami clan. He routinely supplied his men with horses that were ordinarily considered rejects because of their color or coat, and instead of drilling his men on a parade ground he would lead fifty or a hundred of them into the field and practice riding skills. They charged to and fro and dismounted at a full run. Because of this, they became very famous and everyone was terrified to face them.

As far as a horse's size, it is appropriate that the horse be the proper size to the stature of the warrior. If one can only afford a single horse, it should be tall and strong with good stamina and disposition for the desired use.

A warrior can love his horse or view him as an undesirable necessity. Ancient warriors highly valued their horses because a good horse allowed them to move about while dressed in heavy armor as though they were using their own feet. These warriors cared for their horses—they tended to their wounds, fed and brushed them daily, and wept when they died.

These days, warriors only buy faulty horses to train them and sell them for a profit. In this they are no better than merchants. It would be better if they never owned a horse.

THE IMPORTANCE OF A GOOD SENSEI

In order to claim the title of warrior, one must select a qualified martial-arts sensei to teach him the secrets of the art of war and bring him to the highest level of martial-arts skill. Some say that it is a waste of time for a young warrior to study martial arts and military affairs, but this is a completely false assumption on their part. In every age, warriors have risen from nowhere to become famous generals and defenders of nations, and many of them accomplished tremendous deeds.

Since this happened in times past, it is very likely that it will happen again.

The study of the martial arts will sharpen the intellect of the brilliant and help those who are slow to improve their mental ability. Therefore, every warrior should make the study of martial arts his top priority.

A warrior who is not properly grounded will grow arrogant and think himself better than he really is and look down on others. He will start spouting silly ideas as reasonable theory and prop himself up as a teacher, thus misleading many young warriors. They seek fame and profit and after a while they can no longer call themselves warriors. This comes from receiving only half the needed knowledge and humility from their martial-arts sensei.

Study the martial arts with a wholehearted approach and never settle for anything less. Practice until you reach enlightenment and you will have completed the circle, ending up where you started, and you will be at peace with your skills. If you practice with only a halfhearted effort you will never reach enlightenment nor will you ever gain the confidence you need. You will lose touch with reality and become confused by the fantasy of martial arts and may well lead others astray also.

When I say that you will end up where you started I mean that you will release your mind from the content of the martial arts and so return to the ease of mind you had before starting the study, because you will be completely at one with your knowledge and skill in the process of martial arts.

Those who do not reach this level are like improperly seasoned food reeking of imperfection. A halfhearted warrior reeks of pretentiousness.

Section Two:
Keeping Your Home in Order

THE PROPER WAY

If a warrior and his wife are in disagreement over something he should sit down with her and explain his concerns calmly so that she will understand. If the disagreement is over some small thing, it is best to forgive her and drop the subject.

If the dispute is grievous and you cannot reach agreement, you may divorce her and send her back to her parents, but this is only for extreme circumstances.

The warrior should see his wife as the honor of his life and the lady of his home. It is unacceptable to raise your voice or swear at her, and only a complete coward would dare threaten his wife with a weapon or strike her with his hand. A female warrior who was raised in a warrior home would not for one second tolerate such behavior if she were a man. But because she is a woman and weaker she has no choice put to put up with it no matter how many tears she may shed.

A true warrior would never prey on weaker individuals or act as a bully. One who does such things is not a true warrior but an absolute coward.

YOUR NEPHEW

For ordinary people the title of nephew is used for sons of your brother, younger or older, and for sons of your sister, even though she is married into another family. Most people treat all of their nephews the same, but for the warrior there is a difference.

The son of your elder brother, since he is the heir who will carry on the family name, should be treated the same as your brother. Although you may have many nephews that you treat with ordinary courtesy, the son of your elder brother is due extra reverence.

As far as your sister's sons, even though they are your nephews, you should treat them with the courtesy and respect due someone from another family, because even though they are related to you, they are also members of a different family with a different name.

Likewise, if a nephew, younger brother, or even your own son is adopted into another family in order to carry on their family name, it is important to treat them as strangers from the other family. Otherwise, if you still treat them as your son or brother, the family who adopted him will wonder why you allowed them to adopt him in the first place. Now, if the adopting family is mistreating your son, brother, or nephew, it is perfectly acceptable for you to provide for them.

If a father allows his daughter to marry into another family and her husband dies after a son is born and your grandson will assume the head of the house, it is best to let the dead husband's family make nine out of ten decisions concerning the life of the child.

If the husband lives, but is very poor, it is acceptable to help your daughter with money. But if the family is wealthy it is best to stay out of their private affairs.

If someone from your own family or house falls into destitution it is your duty to look after him or her until the family is reestablished.

A warrior should never respect the rich or disrespect the poor simply because of their financial situation. It is proper to treat a respectable person with respect and a dishonorable person with contempt regardless of money.

This is the way of the warrior.

BUDGETING

A warrior should always be careful with his money, regardless of his income, in order to insure that he is always able to properly care for his family.

If a warrior on a fixed income finds out that he has overspent and is going into debt, he can still recover if he immediately changes his spending habits and cuts back wherever he can. By simplifying his life, he will regain a sound footing in a short time, because by cutting back he will create a surplus.

If a lower-ranking warrior, who is already on the edge, tries to live in a style beyond his means by giving in to unchecked desires, he will quickly go broke and no amount of cutting back will save him because he needs all of his income just to survive.

A warrior should keep his personal finances a private matter. Keep in mind that he is required to maintain certain equipment fitting his rank and station, as are his colleagues, and there is nothing that can be done about this. If one is not careful he may fall into debt and begin to say and do things that he should not and damage his reputation, all because of a misuse of money.

A warrior should plan his finances from the beginning and live according to his means. He should avoid unnecessary expenses and buy only what is necessary for living. This is known as the way of budgeting.

On the other hand, let us consider this: regardless of income, if a warrior is consumed with the idea of saving money, he may have a large savings but his standard of living will suffer. Needed repairs on equipment or household items will go undone and he may become the slave of money and gain a reputation as a greedy miser.

This may be acceptable for commoners or merchants, but it is contemptible for a warrior. If one disdains spending worthless money, how likely is it that he will lay down his life?

As it is written, "A miser and a coward are the same."

A MODEST HOUSE

A warrior having a house built in the fief should make sure the outer gate, the landscaping, the front of the house, and the greeting room are all decorated and plush as is befitting a person of his rank. Many people will come and go past the house, so it is important to make a good impression. If everything is well kept and appears prosperous, it will reflect well on the lord.

As far as the living area of the house, it does not need to be ornate; in fact, just to keep the rain out is good enough. This is because in times of war a lord is constantly under the threat of siege, and houses closer to the edge of the city will usually get burned down. This makes it senseless to spend exorbitant amounts of money on the construction.

With this in mind, it is wise for a warrior, even in times of peace, to refrain from sinking everything he has into a building as though he will live there forever. In case of fire, one should have the funds set aside to construct at least a modest living area for his family. Those who have wasted all of their money on an elaborately-constructed building are rightly called fools.

COMBAT READINESS

It is incumbent upon every warrior to maintain the proper armor and weapons for his rank. In addition, each lord has his own rules concerning the proper placement and wearing of family crest, and the posting of flags and banners. Each warrior is individually responsible for compliance and conformity to these rules.

It is unacceptable to run around at the last minute trying to insure compliance with known regulations. A man who is killed by his own side because they could not identify him is killed by his own negligence.

As far as men under your command, it is the duty of the commander to ensure conformity in equipment, weapons, and uniforms. Hold surprise inspections of your troops and make sure their captains are using their budget properly. There may be those who are misusing the money and arming their warriors with wooden or bamboo swords, thinking that war will never come; or they may not issue their troops loincloths, thinking that there is no reason for them to gird up their hakama.

Any warrior who receives pay for services and fails to keep his equipment in proper working order, regardless of how peaceful the times may appear, is one hundred percent responsible for his own demise, unlike the young warrior who is issued no sword or loincloth. The fear of public shame alone should be enough to compel every warrior's compliance.

As a young warrior sets out to purchase his first set of armor, there are a few suggestions that he should heed. If he only has three gold pieces to spend, he should use two-thirds of it for a good helmet and body armor and spend what is left on undergarments, hakama, kimono, coats, fans and various other items of field equipment. Do not make the mistake of buying heavy, ornate armor simply because you are young and strong, because as you grow older it becomes useless. And if you are ever wounded on the battlefield, even light armor can wear you down and become cumbersome.

It is important to keep in mind that if you start with heavy banners and showy emblems you will become known by them and it will be very difficult to do away with them later when they hinder you. Also, one's helmet should be strong and sturdy as, if fate dictates, it may end up in the enemy's camp and it is all you will be judged by.

ATTENDANTS

As a young warrior, you cannot afford a big entourage, because you can arm them with only a single spear and if that should break they would have to attach the spearhead to a stick or bamboo shaft. You should have only as many men as you can properly care for.

You should also insure that your attendants have some type of reliable long sword, even if it is worn or chipped. Supply them with whatever type of clothing they may need as well as a good helmet and body armor. Even if you are very poor, you must provide your attendants with some type of protective wear. You never know where the heart of valor beats, and if you give them a chance you will find courageous warriors in surprising places.

When fighting, it is common for a sword to chip or take damage, so you should see to it that one of your servants carry a replacement. In this situation, you should pass your damaged blade on to a trusted servant, and he can in turn pass his down. This way everyone will have the best weapon available to them, even the most junior.

A WARRIOR'S CALLING

A warrior serves society by standing against evil doers, putting down rabble-rousers, and protecting the weaker members of the populace. Regardless of your rank or skill, you must never raise your hand against a weaker or helpless person, or do any injustice against anyone.

Do not extract more then is reasonable from farmers or order things and fail to pay for them. You should not keep merchants waiting long for their money. A warrior should not lend money to anyone for interest, nor borrow money and pay interest.

Always consider the situations of others; treat farmers under your care kindly and insure that artisans are given reasonable treatment in business. If you find yourself in debt so that you cannot pay it off all at once, at least pay what you can every so often to keep your debtors from doubting your intentions.

It is the duty of a warrior to uphold justice, so it naturally follows that he must never commit any injustice.

MODESTY

As recently as fifty or sixty years ago, *ronin* who were looking for employment would use phrases like, "I must care for at least one spare horse," which was their way of saying that they needed a little more than 500 koku[1] of rice per year. If he said, "I need at least one saddle," it was his way of saying he needed 300 koku of rice per year. If he said, "I must carry at least a secondhand spear," it was his way of saying that he needed at least 100 koku of rice per year.

Until recently, these manners and customs of warriors were still in use, because no warrior wanted to ask for a specific amount of income. Remember the saying, "A starving hawk will not eat grain, and a starving warrior will pick his teeth."

Young warriors did not speak of private matters of gain or loss, and they never mentioned prices. They would blush when hearing of personal matters such as love or sex.

Even though these goals are lofty and out of the reach of most, it is still important to strive toward them. And although we may not reach perfection, always remember, "A bent nose still serves us well."

FRIENDS

For an active warrior, it is important to select only a few of the most brave, righteous, wise, and persuasive as friends from his many peers. There are not many warriors like this, and if you are able to find one

---

1.   A koku is about five bushels, enough to feed one adult for a year.

out of all of your peers, it is enough. You can depend on him in times of need.

As far as warriors making friends with any person they desire with no thought to selection, this is unacceptable.

For a warrior to accept someone as a close friend requires more than hanging around with each other eating and drinking. A warrior must be sure of another person's heart before becoming close to him. Otherwise, if you choose your friends based only on having a good time, you may end up dismissing all formality, speaking loosely, and drinking all night singing puppet-show tunes. In these relationships, where formality is relaxed, it is common that they start to quarrel over minor things and end up not speaking. Rather than seeking a counselor to bring all matters out into the open, they may ignore obvious problems and try to resume their relations.

Although people like these may appear to be warriors, they are really no more than field hands.

GUARD YOUR REPUTATION

It is proper for a warrior to have a reputation for being dependable. With this in mind, it is foolish for a warrior to let himself get caught up in problems that are none of his business or to get involved in others' affairs without being invited. One who does such things is known as a nosy meddler.

Regardless of the circumstances, one should keep his opinion to himself until everyone involved has asked him for his advice, no matter how obvious the answer seems. Remember that, as a warrior, your words have power and you are bound by your very life to even the smallest commitment. Once committed, a warrior cannot stop any-where short of fulfillment, no matter how difficult the situation may become. It is more fitting for a warrior to lay down his life for his lord or family than over some trivial matter.

Earlier generations of warriors would carefully consider every aspect of a situation before agreeing to get involved, and if it seemed hopeless, they would boldly refuse their assistance from the beginning. This is why earlier warriors had solid reputations for finishing what they started. Even the things they agreed to they would thoroughly think through, considering all of the various possibilities so that once commitment was made they would be ready to go to any length to fulfill their obligation. If you are the type of person who agrees to anything for the sake of another's feelings, you will soon gain a reputation as a do-nothing person with half-hearted discipline.

Speaking your opinion, especially if it is contrary, should come from a position of self-discipline and consideration. However, if you are speaking to someone under your authority or a near kinsman you may speak from a more relaxed position. But never forget the power of a warrior's words. Strive to speak only condensed wisdom.

When asked for your opinion, it is better to refuse on the grounds that the subject is beyond your understanding than it is to meekly par-ticipate, giving way to others that you know are wrong. If you are going to offer your opinion, do so with conviction and force of speech. If you give in simply for the sake of conformity, you will eventually become known as a useless adviser.

Once you have spoken your mind, if those in counsel with you do not have the foresight to see the wisdom of your position, or are so arrogant as to insist on their own way as the only way things can get done, you should separate yourself from their decisions, as they will eventually become known as fools.

RELATIONS WITH THE DISAGREEABLE

As an active warrior, you may find yourself ordered to work with someone with whom you have previously cut off all contact. In such a case, you should go straight to the other person's home and have a meeting with him. Make it clear that you have received orders to work with them in such or such a function, and let him know that you wish to resume relations for the sake of efficiency.

If the person is to be your senior at the new post, say something like, "I know you are very experienced in this job, and I would like to know that I can rely on you for instruction and advice. Let us have open and cordial communication so that I can do a good job for you. If tomorrow one of us is reassigned, we can continue not speaking, but while we're working together, we must put personal feelings aside."

This is the way of the warrior, and it goes doubly for one's peers whom he has no ill feelings toward. Keep open and friendly relations with everyone you work with and you will be much more effective. Keep in mind that there are sometimes contentious, power-hungry manipulators who look for any little mistake, even from new, untrained workers, to make fun of, because doing so makes them feel more secure. In combat, these are the types of people who will betray their own men and take credit for the deeds of others.

Avoid them.

PREPARE FOR DEATH

Every warrior should continually read the writings and stories of great warriors from prior times in order to sharpen his fighting spirit and strengthen his resolve to accomplish some great act of valor.

In the illustrious battle records of Takeda Shingen, Oda Nobunaga, and Toyotomi Hideyoshi there are many low-ranking warriors whose names are forever recorded because of some outstanding act of valor. These records also recorded the number of deaths in each battle, and among the dead were many who were high-ranking and respected. It is surprising that these respected warriors were not also recognized for some distinguished act in battle, but valor knows no rank, and only true heroes are remembered.

Whether of low or high rank, every warrior feels the same pain when his head is cut off, so one should thoroughly consider how he wants to be remembered. The goal of every warrior should be that when his time comes to die, he will face his end in a way so brave and heroic that it stuns his friends and foes alike, so that his lord and commanders grieve his death, so his name lives on in legend and his deeds become mythical.

The coward hides behind his friends when attacking and is the first to run away from the fight. He uses his comrades as shields from archers and if he is hit by chance, he will be walked over by his own troops. One like this deserves a dog's death, for as precious as life is he commits such detestable acts.

Think this through. Commit to study acts of bravery and valor and emulate them. Do not cast your life away as a coward would. One way or another, death will come. Determine now how you will face it.

RESPECT ACCOMPLISHMENT, AVOID FOOLISHNESS

It has long been understood that the things a warrior says can come back to haunt him or his family. One never knows where he will be or whom he may need to rely on in the future, so it is best to mind carefully one's words.

Remember that there is a big difference between someone who boasts and someone who criticizes. During times of war, there were those who earned big reputations in battle, and men such as Okubo Hikozaemon and Matsudaria Kagaemon, both working as the shogun's color guard, who boasted of their accomplishments. In those days, every commander had such men under his authority.

Now these were men of action—they did not understand nor care to learn political correctness, and thus they were kept out of the inner circles of social power. Even though these warriors had grand reputations and performed heroic exploits, and were unequaled in the practice of bushido, their positions in salary were much lower than would be expected.

This caused many to have a bitter attitude toward those in power, and they would speak their minds freely about this. Because of their legendary status as warriors, the lords and commanding officers were willing to overlook their conduct, and this empowered them to speak even more loudly and forcefully.

The boasters of today can hardly claim any merit from which to boast, as they have never even donned armor in battle. They sit around drinking and gossiping with their friends and criticize everyone over them, even fellow warriors. These see themselves as superior to others based on nothing but their own imaginations. The boasters of old times had something to boast about, but these today only criticize others. They are fools and do not deserve to be placed in the same category with brave warriors.

TRAVELING

A young warrior of low status may have to ride a packhorse when on a journey. He should tie his swords firmly at the hilt with a string to ensure that they do not come loose in case he falls from the horse, or should hold them in such away as to keep them secure. In either case, it is unadvisable to wrap the hilts of your swords in a thick cloth, because they become useless, and since your banners or baggage is marked with your lord's emblem, you will bring criticism upon the entire house.

It is common these days for riders to trade horses at the discretion of the leader. If the other riders are warriors, it is best to wait until the order is given and the others dismount before dismounting yourself. Otherwise, if you dismount and no one is willing to trade, you appear presumptuous and foolish, and you will be forced to mount the same horse you just got off.

A poem goes:

> Why do you think
> A dangerous shortcut is quickest?
> The fastest route indeed
> May be the longest.

The meaning of this poem is that on a journey one should pay an expert for guidance. If you go it alone thinking that you know best and get hurt, or lose or damage the cargo, you will have no excuse for your foolishness, but if you hire and rely on a guide, it is his responsibility.

MIND YOUR WORDS

A warrior is never to engage in slander or gossip about other warriors, no matter what he has heard or seen with his own eyes. No man is perfect and everyone has faults, including you. Consider the blunders and misunderstandings you have caused over time.

It is a mistake to look at famous or high-ranking warriors as faultless, and if you resent that they are not perfect and slander them, you are really slandering the lord who appointed them. In this way you slander your own master. Understand that the lord surely knew these flaws when he appointed them, but if he waited for flawless men he would never appoint anyone.

How embarrassing it would be for you to need the assistance of a warrior you have criticized. In such a case you will have to swallow your pride, go before him with trembling knees, bow down on the floor before the very man you have insulted, and beg for mercy.

Focus on your own actions, watch your words, and never slander anyone behind their back.

DEALING WITH AN HEIR

During times of war, if a warrior died a heroic death in battle or was injured so that he died thereafter, it was customary for the lord, out of respect, to give the fallen warrior's title and position to his son, even if he was a newborn.

If the child was too young for service as a warrior, the responsibility of guardianship often fell to the deceased warrior's younger brother, if he was not actively employed. In such cases, one should raise his nephew as his own son and provide for his training and education. It is wise, before assuming the position of guardian, to inventory your brother's belongings in the presence of witnesses and record everything in a journal.

When the child reaches the age of fifteen, one should remind the lord in a written letter that the child's sixteenth birthday is coming up. Request that he be allowed to assume his father's position with full pay and benefits.

Now it may be that the lord will grant this request, or he may ask you to continue to look after the youth because of his inexperience. You should refuse this request, no matter how you are pressed, until your petition is granted. At this point, bring your brother's entire inventory and hand it over to his son.

If you are ordered to remain responsible for the youth, you should insist that the young man is given the entire income due his post instead of receiving a portion yourself. Express your concern that the partial income will not be enough to fulfill the responsibilities of the house. Once this is done, seek early withdrawal.

This is the proper way of a guardian, but there are those who are greedy and dishonest. This type of person may cling to power as long as he can and, forced to bequeath the position to the heir, may leave the youth in debt or the estate badly in need of repair. This type of man is a crook and has no morals.

SMILE AT DEATH

The main concern for every warrior, regardless of rank or social position, is how he will face the last few minutes of his life. Whatever your reputation in life, no matter how smart or famous you may have been, if you grovel in the face of death and bring shame on yourself you'll be despised forevermore. Every warrior who has ever achieved heroic status in battle has done so because he placed his life second to his honor.

Accept your death with determination. If your opponent bests you, in your last second of life before he takes your head, look him in the eye, proudly announce your name and smile at him. Show no fear. Do not flinch or cower. If you are mortally wounded, maintain proper discipline as long as you are conscious. Give a report to your superiors and answer any questions from officers or commanders. Carry out your duties then find a comfortable place and wait calmly for death.

In times of peace such as these, should a warrior, young or old, acquire a terminal illness he should face his end with the same resolve. Whether high or low ranking, he should offer his thanks for the kindness he has received from his lord and commander and tell them of his impending death. He should then call all of his friends and family around and apologize for dying in this manner but explain that it is unavoidable. Encourage the young warriors to serve the lord with all loyalty and bravery. Tell them that if they fail in their duty that you will be ashamed of them from the grave. This is the best way to die of an illness.

As it is written, "Let your final words show strength." Do not be the kind of person who is terrified to die, insisting you are getting better even though you are getting worse. Do not take joy simply because someone says you are looking better, and become depressed when others speak of your serious condition. Do not argue with doctors or plead for the sympathy of others.

Take the time to prepare your final words and encourage those around you. As you get close to the end, resolve not to die the useless death of an animal. A warrior who cannot face death in illness will not find an honorable death in battle either. A true warrior will face his end with calculated resolve regardless of how it comes.

Remember what I said at the beginning of this book about keeping death ever in your mind. Do not be so foolish as to watch others die all around you and think that you will live forever.

A warrior only has one chance to die, and he should prepare his entire life to do so with honor.

Section Three:
In the Service of the Lord

FINANCES OF THE FIEF

In the course of daily service, a warrior may find that the fief has run into financial difficulties and that the lord must reduce one's pay for a time to keep the fief running. This cutback may last for several years but, regardless of the amount, a warrior should never complain or criticize his lord, even in the privacy of his own home, much less to strangers.

For a long time now, it has been customary for the warriors to help the lord in times of distress in order to secure the fief, just as the lord helps individual warriors when they are in need of assistance. The lord's private financial straits may also affect his ability to properly fulfill his duties and cause him to live below the standard of his peers. Every warrior who sees his lord subdued by finances is sure to have a heavy heart.

No matter one's financial standing, everyday life continues, and it could well be that your unit is called into action faraway from home because of some disturbance. In such a case, the first priority is to make sure there's enough money to fulfill the order. No matter how crafty one may be, no one can produce money out of thin air, so if you are caught unprepared you'll be like a man who had a boulder dropped on his hand, immobile. For a coordinated effort, the date is set and everyone prepares and sets out to the destination. If you are unprepared, you'll simply have to go with what ever meager supplies you may have on hand.

In peaceful times there's nothing quite as exciting as a military parade. All warriors don their best and put on a show of the fief's might, and all the people, both rich and poor, crowd together to see the spectacle. Now, if it happens that your unit is worn and tattered and appears inferior to others, it will cause a lifetime of shame to the lord and his commanders.

When you look at it this way, it is much better to prepare beforehand, even if it requires every warrior to give back a part of their salary, whatever each can afford.

During this time, you live on a decreased budget and it is important for you to cut back anywhere you can. Use fewer personal servants, wear cheaper clothing, and eat cheaper rice and miso soup, morning and evening. Draw your own water, cut your own firewood, and let your wife cook the food. Endure every hardship without complaint and set your mind on restoring the fief. This is basic nature for the warrior.

During these times do not take leave, but accept any additional duty with all joy. Pawn your extra sword or your wife's luxury items, if necessary. Absorb expense without borrowing money.

At any rate, never criticize your lord for hard times, because even if he never hears of it you will gain a bad reputation among your superior officers.

TWO KINDS OF SERVANTS

Once a warrior has sworn allegiance to a lord, he must no longer regard his life or his body as his own. Every lord has two types of servants under his command, low-end helpers and warriors.

These helpers receive small salaries even though they work hard all day and into the night, because they are never required to die in the service of the lord. They are not required to train or show martial prowess, and even if they run away from an enemy, it is not considered a disgrace. They basically sell their labor for food.

A warrior, on the other hand, has sworn his life to his lord's service. He would rather give up his very life than show cowardice, and will die to protect his lord. A warrior will not retreat a single inch, and the higher his rank the more resolve he will have to live up to his position. For this reason, the warrior receives higher salary even though he does not labor his life away.

The shogun requires each lord to keep a ready reserve according to the size of his fief. A fief of 100,000 koku is required to have 170 horsemen, 60 archers, 350 riflemen, and 150 spearmen at the disposal of the regional commander, besides that which he needs to protect his fief. This is why so many warriors are kept on salary even though there is no war.

A family of warriors in the service of a lord for many generations of peace has received a lot of kindness from the lord even though they have done nothing. In every clan there are those who are slow or dim-witted but the lord provides for them nonetheless. In times of distress each warrior is expected to remember the kindness of his lord to his family and to live up to his duty to the point of death.

In times of peace, a warrior's duties include guard duty, escort, messenger, and even errand boy. Even though these seem mundane, it is important to remember that at any moment an emergency may arise. In such a case, the mundane would quickly turn to the highest duties of the warrior, such as leading an advance, protecting one's lord or commander with his life, or standing alone against a multitude of opponents, calling only on God as a witness to his heroic death.

For these reasons, it is necessary to resign your life to your lord the moment you claim the title of warrior. Keep yourself ready at all times. Practice the martial arts, avoid overeating or drinking, and flee from sexual impurity. A warrior should be disgusted at the thought of dying in his bed and horrified at the thought of dying in some useless quarrel. Watch your words and never engage in silly arguments. Once two warriors get into a heated argument, it is inevitable that blood will flow. Keep inflammatory opinions to yourself and remain determined from the beginning to avoid useless contention. Always remember that your life does not belong to you and you will be careful not to throw it away.

PREPARATION AND CONSTRUCTION

An active warrior has two main areas of service to his lord, preparation for battle and the construction of fortifications.

In many countries there are continuous battles here or there and the warrior must remain ever on guard. In every battle there is a need to construct such things as forts, moats, barricades, and so forth. During this time, every warrior, regardless of rank, must work quickly and without stopping until these things are finished.

In times of peace there's no need to erect fortifications, and every warrior is assigned various other duties by his commander. After a time, some begin to look at these peacetime activities as their primary duty and never consider battle or construction in their wildest dreams. Then, when called upon to build some grand construction, they whine and complain about the work and personal expenses as though they were asked to participate in some great injustice, even though this is and always was their primary duty.

Some even find the daily task of service troublesome and feign illness in order to pawn their responsibility off on others with no consideration for them. These constantly shirk their duties and hide from work with no shame over the contempt of their peers. Others will fulfill their duty but will grumble and complain about having to run errands twice in one day to the same place, or about the condition of the weather. Because of their lazy attitude and weak spirit, they are no more than peasants in a warrior's skin.

In times of war, warriors are expected to endure sweltering heat in the summer, freezing cold in the winter, rain, snow, sleeping out in the open with nothing but their armor for a pillow, and eating only cheap rice and soup. These things they endured whether in open battle, conducting a siege, or defending a fortification. Considering that the same is expected of every warrior, the peacetime hardships are really nothing at all. If one cannot endure in peace he will never hold up in war.

Consider our peacetime luxuries, such as mosquito netting, warm clothes, blankets, and an unlimited choice of foods both morning and night. Count your blessings and stand firm to fulfill your little responsibilities like guard duty or acting as a bodyguard.

Remember the master archer of Kai who hung this maxim on his wall, "Forever in battle."

THE LORD'S CREST

If a warrior receives from his lord a gift of an overcoat or kimono with the lord's family crest on it, he should only wear it in conjunction with his own family crest. It would be disrespectful to wear only the lord's crest, as it would appear that you are a close relative. This would be disrespectful to your own family as well as the lord's.

In time, as the garment grows old and is no longer usable, you should either burn it or cut the lord's crest off. It would be unseemly for the material to be used again in some irreverent fashion with the crest still attached. This could cause one disfavor or illness.

Now, whenever someone is ill or distressed you should make it a point to remain solemn and quiet in their presence, even if you don't know them. Otherwise you may gain a reputation as a heartless person.

THE PROPER WAY TO ACCEPT AN ASSIGNMENT

When in daily service a warrior is appointed a job such as assassin, it is important that he accept the job in all joy and gratitude. For one man to be singled out from all other warriors is indeed a high honor, and you should be very grateful and accept the task with enthusiasm. To accept it in a halfhearted manner is disgraceful.

Consider this, you may set out to complete your task with determination and bravery, mustering your spirit to do a good job for the lord, but life and death is often decided by Heaven and you may be wounded or killed by the man you were sent to cut down. In such a case, you will certainly be judged by your peers afterward for either good or evil.

If you are successful, people will say that you were determined from the beginning and nothing could have stood in your way. If you fail they will say that you seemed strong in the beginning but somehow lost heart and failed.

If you accept the job halfheartedly, then no matter how successful you are people will consider your enterprise a matter of luck because you seemed unsure from the beginning. For these reasons, it is important to accept any appointment with firm resolve.

The way of the warrior is to accept failure in nothing, no matter how small. If someone asks you for assistance you should reason it out and consider whether the request is possible or not. If it is, accept it with solid determination. If it is not, refuse it with the same solid determination. If you accept it with halfhearted enthusiasm, it will cause the other person to doubt your sincerity and make him wish he had never asked you in the first place.

If you accept anything with halfhearted determination, you have failed before you even begin.

KNOW YOUR HERITAGE

A warrior should thoroughly study the history and traditions of his clan and be ready to give a detailed account if asked. Young warriors, much less seniors, should know the battle stories and heroes of the fief. If you cannot answer questions about your fief if asked by an outsider, you will gain a reputation as one not committed to his family, no matter how well you do all other things.

ALWAYS PROTECT THE LORD

When guarding one's lord on a journey, it is important to thoroughly study any stopover before the sun sets. Talk to the locals about the roads coming in and out of the area. Know where they lead. Gain a sense of direction based on trees, buildings, fields or temples. Learn the travel conditions ahead and prepare to continue the trip. This way you will be prepared in case of an emergency or fire during the night, and you will be able to lead your lord to safety.

Generally, walk in front of your lord uphill and behind him downhill. Do not look at this as a small thing, because it can be very important. Think about things like these when you are escorting your lord. Make them part of your everyday way of thinking.

THE WAY OF CORRUPTION

The old saying "White shirts and officials are best when new," sounds somewhat silly but it is based in truth.

When a white shirt is new it looks very nice, clean, and bright. After it is worn for a while it starts to fade and grays around the neck and sleeves. After a while, the whole thing is ugly and unusable.

When an official is new, he considers every small part of his job vitally important. He is eager to please his lord and studies the rules of the job, taking to heart his oath of office. He avoids bribes and favors of large gifts and returns a gift for every small gift he receives.

After a while, it is easy for him to accept people's praise in stride and considers his duty commonplace. He will loosen his morals and hint to others that he is open to bribes or large gifts in exchange for favors. He will play between the lines without stating outright his intentions.

In this way, it is easy to see how an official's gradual corruption is the same as the fading of a white shirt.

With a white shirt, one only need clean it with strong soap and it will be clean again. A man's heart, however, is another matter. Once a man has allowed corruption to enter his soul there is no amount of cleaning that will remove it. If a shirt is washed once or twice it may suffice, but a man's heart cannot be cleansed with washing every minute of everyday.

Like the shirt, which has various kinds of cleaning solutions, a warrior's heart can only be cleansed with strict adherence to loyalty, duty, and courage. Loyalty, duty, or courage may clean a warrior's heart, depending on how corrupt he is, but a faithful adherence to all three will surely restore his soul.

THE PROPER USE OF AUTHORITY

A warrior on duty may be said to either borrow or steal his lord's authority. In addition, a lord may lend his authority to a warrior or have it stolen from him.

If a young warrior is sent on an errand, he has no authority or power of his own, but since he is working for the lord, he is granted the lord's authority to get the job done. This is borrowing a lord's authority.

Now let's say that he enjoys the respect given to him by others while he has this authority, and after he completes his task he continues to use that authority for personal gain. This is stealing the lord's authority.

The warrior should have used the lord's authority only to complete the job then set it aside afterwards.

A lord may grant his authority to a warrior for a certain time to complete an extended job. This is the lord lending his authority to a warrior. But if he is not strict in its use, the warrior may continue to use it, and the longer the situation goes unchecked the harder it is to stop. This is having authority stolen from a lord. This situation can bring a lord much disgrace, because soon everyone will start to look to the lord's warrior for permission to do whatever they wish. This will take away from the lord's power and add to the warrior. Everyone will go to the warrior for approval and seek his favor, believing that it is all they need. At this point, others will take the warrior's commands to heart but dismiss the lord's. Then if the lord needs men he will have none to follow his orders.

If the lord trust the warrior and knows nothing about his abuse, others will back away from saying anything out of fear, even if they loathe the situation. People will gossip about it and everyone will see it as harmful to the lord. The lord's cunning will soon be called into question, as he appears not to see what is going on right in front of him.

The warrior may grow bold and start to use the lord's property as his own, entertaining and having parties, and after a while the fief goes into debt.

Remember, warriors are granted a lot of favor and power in their own right. It is unacceptable for one to disrespect the lord by thinking too highly of himself. For this reason, we meditate on the old saying, "A warrior has a lord, but not a self."

PUBLIC OFFICE

A warrior assigned to administer public funds or budget has a very delicate job to undertake, even if he receives special training. On one hand, he must make sure that his lord has all the funds necessary to properly run the fief, but on the other hand, he must not distress the populace or workers living in or around the town.

If one works with only his lord in mind, the populace will suffer, but if he strives to ease the burden of the commoners, the fief administration will suffer. One must equally consider the interest of both of these or one of them will face loss.

Regardless of how wise and talented one may be from the beginning, his mind is easily corrupted by the sickness of greed. And if one has no accountability in the collection or distribution of money, he will naturally begin to grow accustomed to large sums of it. At that point he may start to desire things that are beyond his means and divert official money to buy them. After a while, he will build houses and furnish them with expensive things. A person like this is a thief.

If a warrior replaces proven procedures and methods of financial accounting with new, untested measures, causing hardship on all the people, it does not matter if he is motivated by greed or not, because the result is the same. A person such as this will blindly collect money without regard to the hardship he is causing, because he is focused only on immediate gain. He will rewrite the laws and scheme to gain the approval of his superiors, but when things go wrong he will blame it on the shortsightedness of those same superiors. A person like this is an extortionist.

Now, as far as the thief is concerned, he has conducted himself far below the standard of a warrior. He has stolen and lived lavishly, but he will eventually get caught or face Heaven's punishment. Once such a person is removed from office, no more harm can come. But the extortionist will cause trouble long after he has gone, because he has changed laws and procedures that will affect the fief for years to come. For this reason, he is worse than a thief. Therefore, if a thief is beheaded an extortionist should be crucified.

In old times, the thief and extortionist were looked upon as two different kinds of people, but now they are considered the same. Both of them seek personal gain at the expense of the lord and the populace. These shrewd connivers are the worst of the worst, and if beheading and crucifixion are due to thieves and extortionist, it is difficult to say what punishment is due officials who embody both.

REMEMBER WHERE YOU CAME FROM

A low-ranking warrior quickly learns the moods and characteristics of his supervisors, the personalities of his fellow warriors, and the particulars of the unit as a whole. If he is favored with promotion, he should remember what it was like in the lower ranks and carry out his duties with great concern for his troops; but he should still strive to fulfill the desires of his lord without fear or favor.

Over time, as a warrior is promoted, he may easily forget his troops because his concerns and responsibilities slowly change. In the end he is in a completely different situation, and concern for his troops or diligence to his lord may slip.

Take Sakuma and Uozumi for example. Both were excellent warriors for their clans when low ranking, but after they were promoted they were tossed out and their own arrogance caused their lords to shun them and brought them to ruin.

PROCRASTINATION

For a warrior serving a lord, it is vitally important to complete the day's task before the day's end. The warrior, above all others, knows how uncertain life is, and it is foolish to rely on the future. Do not put off what you can do right now; face up to your responsibilities as they come and when death approaches you will have no regrets.

The trouble comes when a warrior begins to procrastinate and grows lazy and slothful. Rather than facing responsibilities as they arise, he puts them off until the future holds more work than he can do. Since he has already grown lazy, he will dread the mound of work before him and continue to put off even the most pressing matters. After a while, he will make excuses for urgent matters or pawn his work off on others. Before long everyone avoids him, no one trusts him, and his unfinished work grows far beyond his control. All this because he allowed himself to count on tomorrow for time to do what he should have done today.

Take guard duty for example. Every warrior knows his set days well in advance and should be prepared accordingly to show up and assume his post before the time to change the guard. But some put off preparations and sit around smoking with their friends or chatting with their wives until the time for their shifts. When they realize this they jump to their feet and run from their house unprepared. They rush down the street, appearing rude and trying to quickly get to their post. By the time they arrive, late, they are panting and covered with sweat, even in the dead of winter. They offer a multitude of excuses and blame everything under the sun for their tardiness as though everything conspired against them. How foolish. Everyone knows the importance of guard duty, and there is no excuse for showing up late and unprepared.

If you are one who understands this and always shows up on time, be careful not to make a big show of your relief showing up late by pacing about, yawning, and acting as though you cannot stand to spend another second on duty.

KEEP YOUR LORD FIRST

When two lords with their entourage cross paths on a journey or meet at a river crossing, it may happen that their men argue. If the argument grows out of control so that more and more warriors, irrespective of side, become entangled and a struggle arises, it may then happen that the lords get involved. Once the lords are involved, matters can quickly grow out of hand because there is no arbitrator, and thus a whole war may break out over nothing.

For these reasons, it is necessary to realize that the lowest warrior can cause much trouble while on a journey, and it is essential that you carefully consider your actions at all times. Big trouble can come from nowhere, so you should not only look at yourself but your comrades as well to ensure that everyone acts reasonably.

If on a journey to the capital you encounter another lord's vanguard and an argument ensues so that a fight breaks out, you should rush to your lord's armor bearer, get his spear and horse, and bring them close to his side. Be watchful and observant, and if it appears that things are going to get out of hand, help the lord mount his horse and ready his weapon. Then draw your sword and prepare to defend your lord.

If you escort your lord to some social function or party and an unexpected fight breaks out, you should rush inside with your sword in hand and announce to the greeter who you are and whom you are with. Then say that you are concerned for your lord and demand to see him. If the greeter tries to comfort you by saying that all is fine, you should refuse to accept this until you have seen the lord with your own eyes and know that he is safe. After this, you may tell your comrades that all is fine and relax.

DUTY IS ITS OWN REWARD

At times, a warrior may consider some special project assigned to him to have been accomplished extraordinarily well. He may find his peers and even some of his superiors impressed as well and openly complementing him. If in such a situation one's lord fails to recognize his accomplishments with a reward or any other outward sign, it is important not to get discouraged as though his efforts were wasted.

Many in this situation will complain and hold his lord in contempt because of his perceived ingratitude. This is unacceptable for a warrior.

In times of war, the warrior was expected to live in the field daily, to fight when called upon without hesitation, and to lay down his life for his lord or commanders. This was a normal way of life and one would ever boast or expect praise for it. If such humility is expected of heroes, how much more for peacetime warriors who spend their days bowing and rubbing their hands together, their greatest challenge being proper speaking because the idea of battle is far removed. The warrior should remain unchanged whether in times a peace or war. Loyalty is the duty of every warrior no matter the circumstances. Notions of reward or merit are strictly up to the lord. If you receive a reward, do so graciously; but if not, hold your tongue.

EVIL SPIRITS

A warrior owes everything to his lord for the great kindness he has received. Some may think that the only way to repay the lord is to commit seppuku on his death in order to escort him into the afterlife. But this custom is now outlawed, and the idea of spending one's life performing indoor acts of servitude is far from desirable.

So what else is there for one who desires to do some great or heroic thing with his life? If you desire to distinguish yourself above your peers, even if it cost to your life, then direct that desire toward more outstanding service. This is far more desirable than seppuku because it will benefit the lord, fief, and all warriors great and small. A person of this great service is always remembered as one who embodied the attributes of loyalty, faith, and bravery.

Evil spirits always haunt the house of high-ranking warriors, trying to bring about death or destruction.

Death by an evil spirit is a curse brought on a house and is different from ordinary death. Death brought on by an evil spirit comes without warning and strikes someone who will benefit the entire fief because he fully embodies the three main areas of loyalty, faith, and bravery.

Amari Saemon fell from his horse and died while still very young. He was the commander of Takeda Shingen's warriors and many believe that he was killed by a spirit who long haunted the house.

Other evil spirits cause trouble by entering the heart of the lord, his high counselors, or his trusted commanders. These spirits affect the lord by giving him bad advice and causing him to commit evil deeds and rule unjustly. There are six ways that these evil spirits operate.

1. It filters the information that the lord receives to insure that only its views are given consideration. The spirit gains the ear of the lord and finds ways to discredit any good advice that he receives. After a time, the lord gives weight to his advice alone.

2. The spirit watches for promising young warriors and transfers them or assigns them to duty to keep them far away from the lord. They make certain that the lord is surrounded by men under their control so that they can hide extravagant lifestyles from him.

3. The spirit whispers in the lord's ear that he does not have enough descendants and convinces him of its importance. The warrior possessed by the spirit will gather together many beautiful young women, without regard to the quality of their families, and have them dance before the lord as talented musicians play for them. Even the strongest of men would fall under these circumstances, much less those of weaker constitution. After a while, the lord will concern himself with nothing else. The gathering will grow into an all-day drinking party and the lord will fail to administer his duties. The lord will then assign important duties to the counselors and concern himself only with carousing.

4. The counselor must start to spend large amounts of money to keep the lord occupied. As bills accumulate and are paid, the lord remains unaware because his own level of living has not

suffered. Soon, the counselor must hold back pay and rewards of lower-ranking warriors and pay no mind to the distress it causes. In this situation, everyone will hold bitterness in their hearts and no one will remain loyal.

5.   Since the lord is otherwise occupied, matters of the military will be pushed aside. There will be no inspections of warriors or armory storehouses. No one will complain about this, as money is tight and inspections are expensive. After a time, the military will be unprepared to handle any action whatsoever, even though generations of warriors have prided themselves on military readiness.

6.   Living with addictions to these vices will soon destroy the lord's health and cause his warriors to lose heart. Eventually, something will come about to reveal the fief's condition and bring discredit upon the lord.

Everyone will naturally hate this devil that has brought evil upon the fief, but instead of taking the matter into hand they will do nothing but talk behind his back. At best, maybe nine or ten will speak openly of him and testify before the court. It would be better to settle the problem in private rather than drag everything into the open so that it reflects poorly on the whole fief. Once matters are in the open, they are subject to investigation by the government, and if the government gets involved it always ends with the fief's lord being replaced. This would be like killing the ox to fix its horns or burning down a house to kill the rat inside. If the lord is replaced then all those who work for him are dismissed.

It is far better for a single warrior to lay hold of the evil one and run him through, or take his head then commit seppuku. This would settle the matter and keep the lord from open shame. With the evil influence gone, the fief would soon return to a calm and peaceful state. A warrior who would take such matters onto himself to settle it fully embodies loyalty, faith, and courage 100 times more than one who simply follows his lord into death.

WARRIOR REFINEMENT

A warrior, of course, concentrates most of his efforts toward developing strength and power, but if in the end if that is all you have you have failed to grasp the true spirit of bushido. A true warrior concentrates on his education and cultural refinement as well. Study things like poetry or the tea ceremony, even if you have to do it part-time. One who does not study all things will never grasp the meaning of the things that are going on around him or understand the lessons of history regardless of how brilliant he purports to be.

To avoid many obstacles, it is important for you to have a solid knowledge of the ways of other countries as well as a complete understanding of our own history. In all things, give thought to the principles of time, space, and position. Make decisions accordingly and you'll avoid many difficulties. For this reason, every warrior should be diligent in study.

Never rely on your knowledge or education as a crutch to prop up a self-inflated ego. Those who do this tend to look down on others as though they were beneath them. They see everything foreign as modish and consider things of their own country as commonplace. Men like this tend to make judgments based on theory alone without consideration of real-life applications.

Take poetry for example. Throughout our history, great generals and fierce warriors have penned some of the world's greatest poems. It is proper for every warrior, regardless of rank, to master the ability to express his thoughts in a poem. But if one studies poetry exclusively he will grow round and soft. He will lose the warrior's fighting spirit and after awhile will look more like a monk than a warrior. He will lose his martial skill and end up armed with only witty jokes and a sharp tongue. Even in the presence of serious and focused warriors, he will offer nothing but funny stories. This is to be avoided by a warrior.

Learn the rituals of the tea ceremony; it has been a part of warrior culture for a very long time. Even if you have no personal desire to participate in the tea ceremony, it is very likely that you will be invited to participate at some point and you should have an understanding of how to sit, eat, and sip tea, as well as how to enter the room.

The utensils should be plain but functional. Remember that the tea ceremony is a celebration of efficiency and tranquility. It is proper for even the lowest warrior to build a tearoom and practice the tea ceremony in this spirit. However, if one is not careful a spirit of elegance may overtake the spirit of pure efficiency and cause one to seek finer wares. A simple bowl and the cheapest teapot are highly desirable. The value of the ceremony is found in the absence of luxury, and if one is not mindful he will start to desire more and more ornate utensils and older scrolls to hang on his walls.

The spirit of luxury can turn a warrior into nothing more than a merchant, evaluating the worth of everything and bargaining for a slightly better deal. Before long, everything is evaluated on its investment value alone, and the warrior becomes like one seeking profit instead of purity. Rather than this, it would be better to never have known the word "tea" or learned how to sip from a bowl.

It is the purity of the warrior spirit that is important.

From the Author

I hope you enjoyed *The Code of the Warrior* and got a lot out of it. Remember, "It is the purity of the warrior spirit that is important." If you follow the teachings in this book, you will keep your spirit pure. Train hard.

D. E. Tarver

About the Author

D. E. Tarver holds black belts ranging from 2nd to 7th degree in seven different styles of Japanese and Filipino martial arts. He has taught martial arts and strategy for twenty years. Since his honorable discharge from the Marines, he has spent time in Japan and the United States.

0-595-26917-6